The Colours We Eat

Green Foods

Patricia Whitehouse

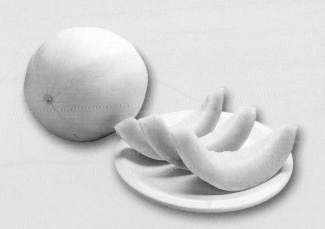

Raintree

www.raintreepublishers.co.uk
Visit our website to find out more information about **Raintree** books.

To order:
☎ Phone 44 (0) 1865 888112
▤ Send a fax to 44 (0) 1865 314091
▭ Visit the Raintree Bookshop at **www.raintreepublishers.co.uk** to browse our catalogue and order online.

First published in Great Britain by Raintree, Halley Court, Jordan Hill, Oxford OX2 8EJ, part of Harcourt Education.
Raintree is a registered trademark of Harcourt Education Ltd.

Editorial: Nick Hunter and Diyan Leake
Design: Sue Emerson (HL-US) and Joanna Sapwell (www.tipani.co.uk)
Picture Research: Amor Montes de Oca (HL-US) and Maria Joannou
Production: Jonathan Smith

Originated by Dot Gradations
Printed and bound in China by South China Printing Company

ISBN 1 844 21605 5
07 06 05 04 03
10 9 8 7 6 5 4 3 2 1

British Library Cataloguing in Publication Data
Whitehouse, Patricia
Green Foods
641.3
A full catalogue record for this book is available from the British Library.

Acknowledgements
The publishers would like to thank the following for permission to reproduce photographs: Craig Mitchelldyer Photography pp. **20L**, **20R**, **21**, **23** (salad); Dwight Kuhn pp. **4**, **8**, **12**, **23** (leaves, pod), back cover (pod); E. R. Degginger p. **11**; Fraser Photos p. **19** (Greg Beck); Heinemann Library (Michael Brosilow) pp. **1**, **5**, **6**, **16**, **17**, **18**, **22**, **23** (avocado), **24**; Rick Wetherbee pp. **10**, **23** (vine); Visuals Unlimited pp. **7** (Rob and Ann Simpson), **13**, **14** (John D. Cunningham), **15** (David Siren), **23** (Brussels sprouts, David Siren; rind, Rob and Ann Simpson; stem, John D. Cunningham), back cover (watermelon, Rob and Ann Simpson).

Cover photograph of French beans, reproduced with permission of Heinemann Library (Michael Brosilow).

Every effort has been made to contact copyright holders of any material reproduced in this book. Any omissions will be rectified in subsequent printings if notice is given to the publishers.

 CAUTION: Children should be supervised by an adult when handling food and kitchen utensils.

Some words are shown in bold, **like this.** You can find them in the glossary on page 23.

Contents

Have you eaten green foods?

Colours are all around you.

How many different colours can you see in these foods?

All of these foods are green.

Which ones have you eaten?

What are some green fruits?

Some melons are big and green.

Honeydew melons are sweet and juicy.

Watermelons are sweet and juicy, too!

The hard green skin of a watermelon is called the **rind**.

What are some green vegetables?

These cabbages have dark green **leaves**.

Cabbages are good for you.

Lettuce leaves are green, too.

We eat them in **salads**.

Have you tried these juicy green fruits?

Some grapes are green.

Grapes grow on **vines**.

Limes have shiny green skin.

They grow on trees.

Have you tried these green vegetables?

pod

pea

Peas are green and good for you.

They grow inside **pods**.

Brussels sprouts are good for you, too.

They look like little cabbages!

What green parts of plants do we eat?

We eat the **stem** of the celery plant.

Celery is crunchy and is good in **salads**.

We eat the flowers of the broccoli plant.

Broccoli is good for you, too.

Have you tried these soft green fruits?

Kiwi fruit have lots of **seeds** in them.

They are tasty in fruit **salad**.

The inside of an avocado is soft and green.

Sometimes people eat mashed avocados.

What soups and drinks are green?

Pea soup is made by cooking dried peas.

Add fresh peas to make it bright green!

Limeade is a green drink.

It is made by squeezing the juice out of limes.

Recipe: Crunchy Green Salad

❗ Ask an adult to help you.

First, wash some lettuce, celery and cucumber.

Next, cut them into small pieces.

Then, mix the vegetables in a bowl.

Now, eat your crunchy green **salad**!

Quiz

Can you name these green foods?

Look for the answers on page 24.

Glossary

leaves
the flat parts attached to the stem of a plant

pod
case that some beans and peas grow in

rind
hard skin on the outside of a fruit or vegetable

salad
a cold dish made up of chopped fruit or vegetables

seed
the part of a plant that grows into another plant

stem
the main part of a plant which grows from the ground

vine
a plant that has a very long, thin stem

Index

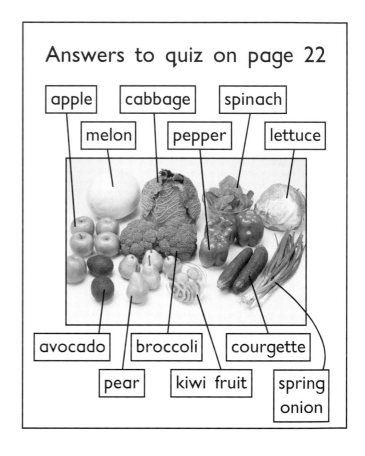

Answers to quiz on page 22

apple · cabbage · spinach · melon · pepper · lettuce · avocado · broccoli · courgette · pear · kiwi fruit · spring onion

24

Titles in the Colours We Eat series include:

Hardback   1 844 21605 5

Hardback   1 844 21606 3

Hardback   1 844 21607 1

Hardback   1 844 21608 X

Hardback   1 844 21609 8

Hardback   1 844 21610 1

Find out about the other titles in this series on our website www.raintreepublishers.co.uk